nickelodeon™

HEY ARNOLD!™

Guide to
Relationships

Written by
Stacey Grant

Contents

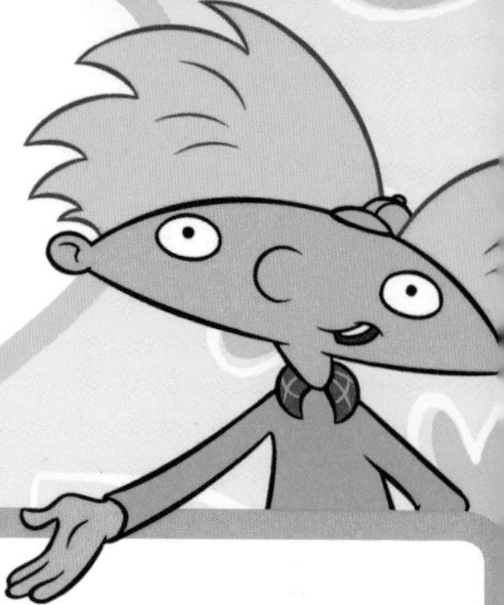

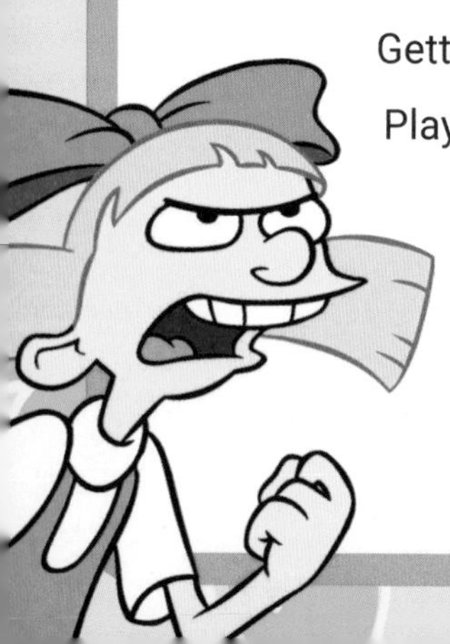

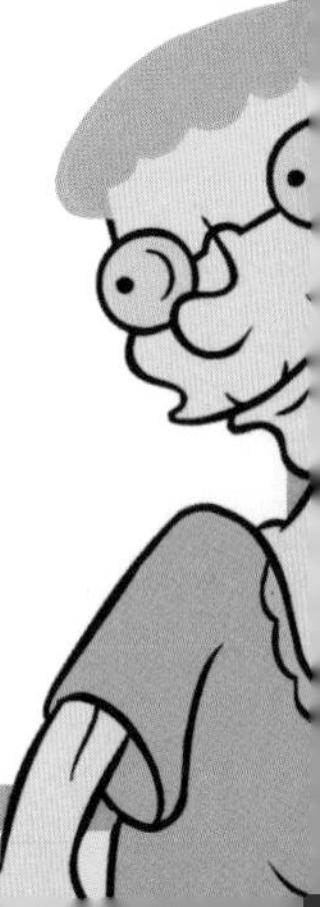

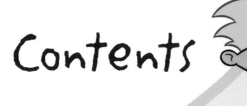

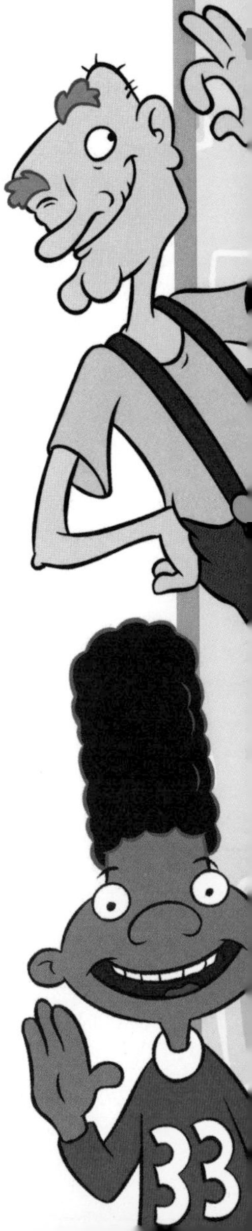
33

Hey, you!

Love is tough—we get it. But if a bunch of fourth graders have more relationship game than you, you've got a problem. Whether you're single with a life-size shrine to your crush in your closet or you're trying to keep your longtime boo from kicking you to the curb, the gang from P.S. 118 have been there, too.

So stop monologuing and let your faves show you how to avoid getting ghosted, act chill around your crush, and get over heartbreak. It might mean some hard truths, but bae's worth it, right?

Start reading, football head.

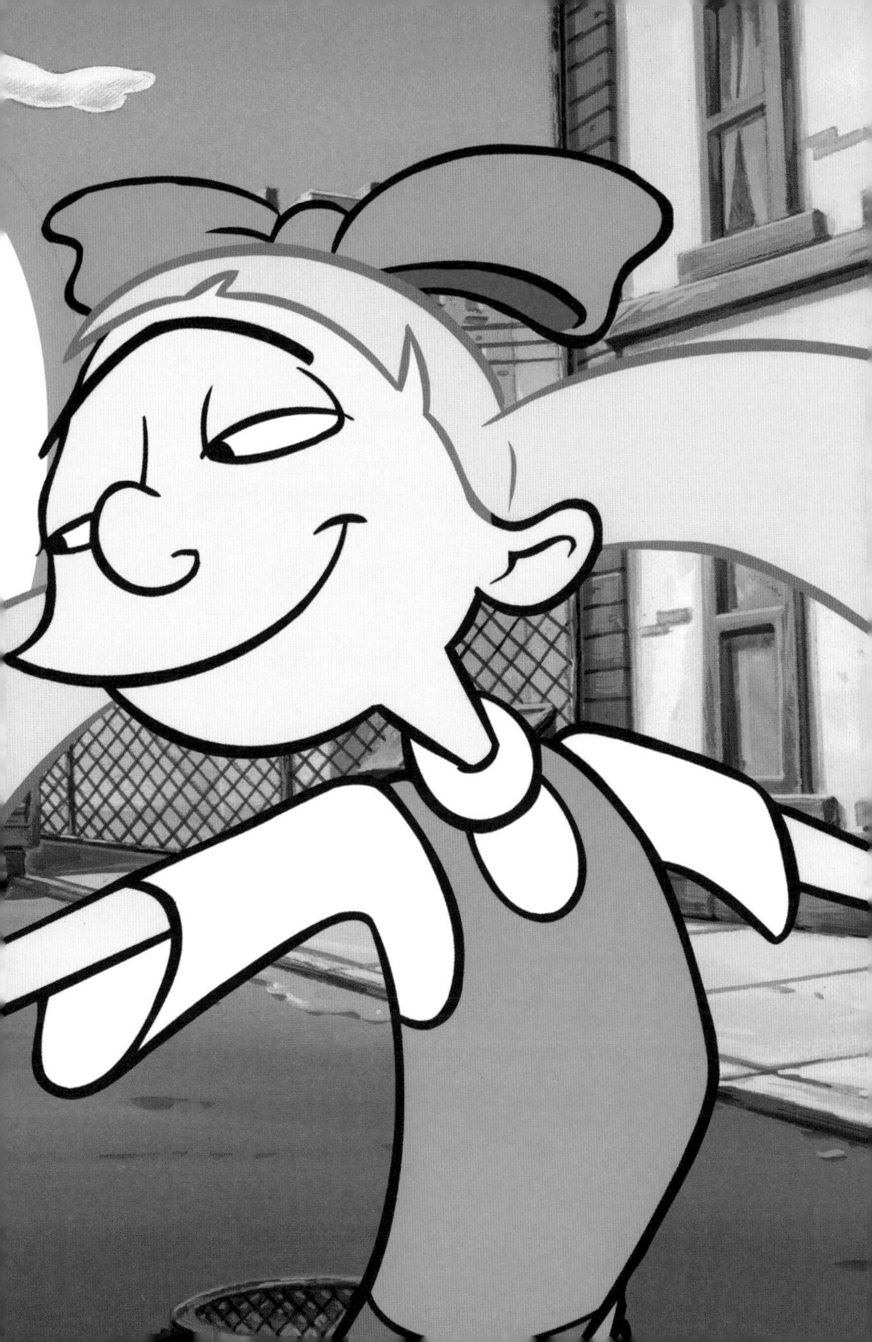

The road to true love

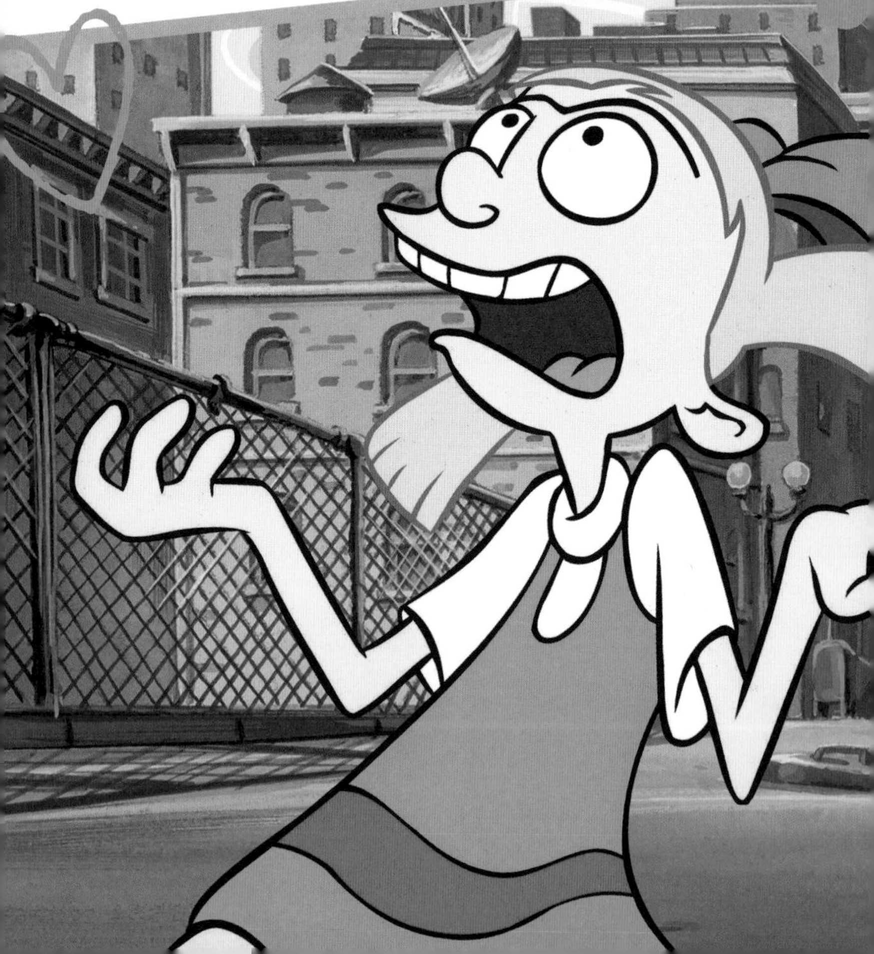

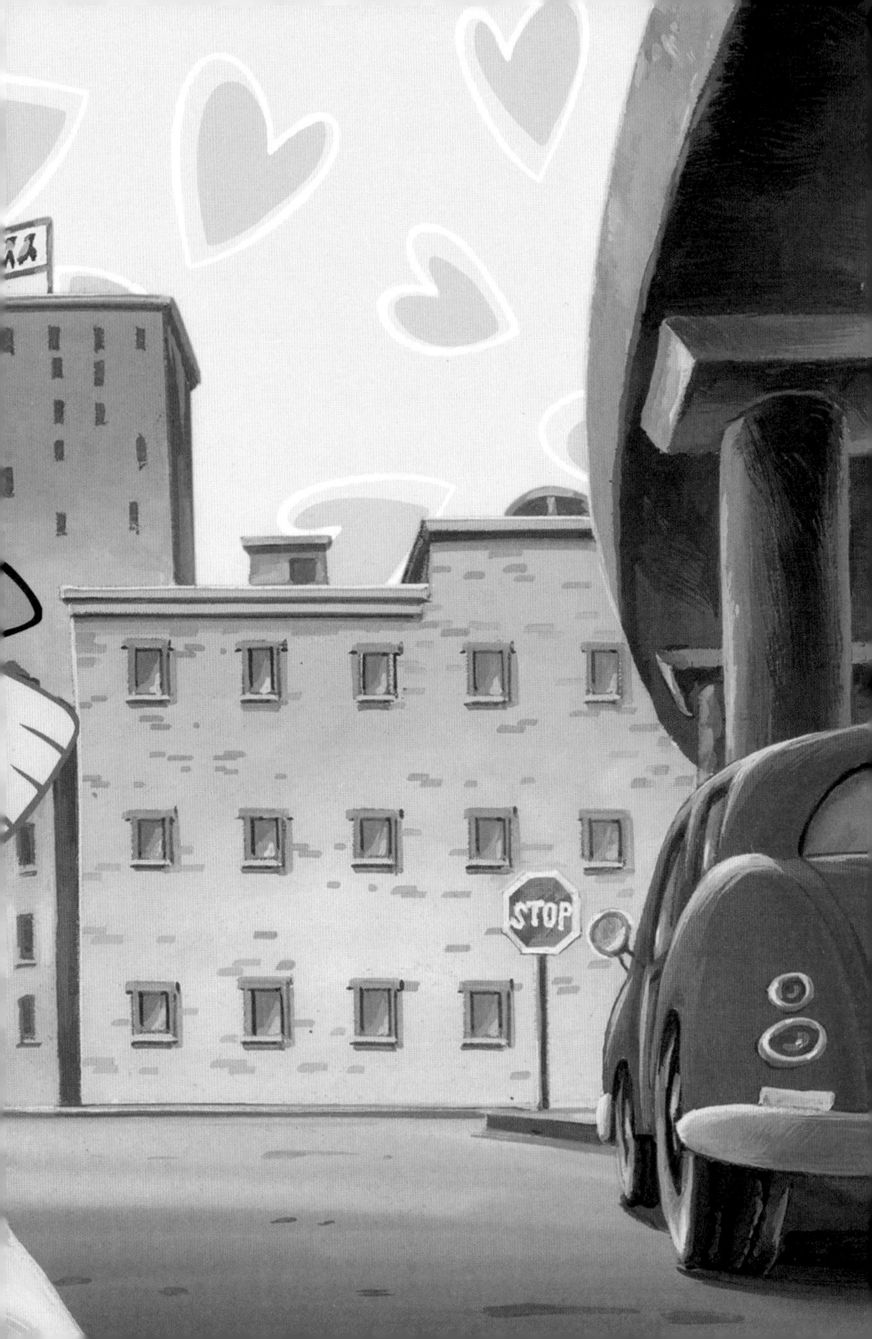
STOP

"Stop it Ma, I'm not charming and I'm not handsome. I'm a big dumb ugly kid."

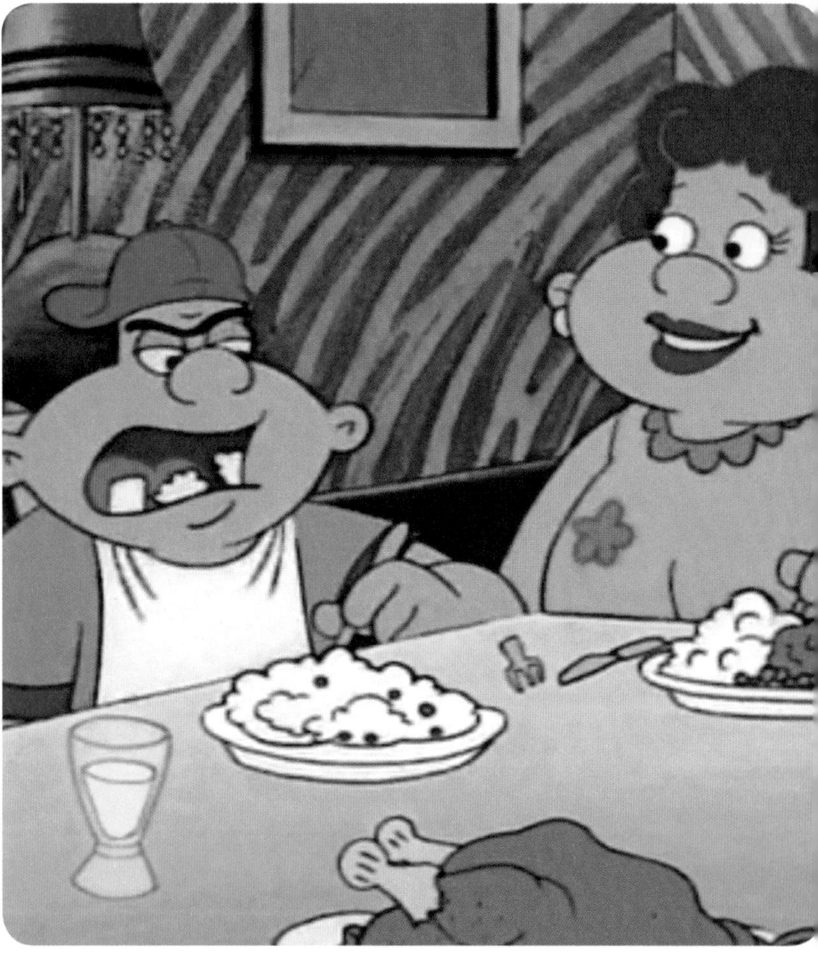

Harold Berman: "Hey Harold!" Season 3, Episode 11 (October 1998)

Learn to love yourself

If you don't love yourself at your worst, then you don't deserve to love yourself at your best. The adult world has as many bullies as the schoolyard. Don't help them out by putting yourself down, too. Trust the voices that raise you up instead.

(Thanks, mom.)

#Slay   #2Cute2B4gotten   #LoveYourBody

First love

Expectation: You're going to end up marrying the first person who stole your heart.
Reality: LOL, not even close.

Odds are your first love isn't going to be your last love, and that's okay. It's good to branch out and meet all the Arnolds, Lilas, Harolds, and Helgas of the world.

#TBT   #PuppyLove   #ChildhoodSweethearts

"I like your bow, because it's pink like your pants."

Arnold Shortman: "Helga on the Couch," Season 4, Episode 16 (December 1999)

"Maybe I should have gone a bit lighter on the eye shadow?"

Helga Pataki: "The Makeover," Season 1, Episode 4 (November 1996)

Own your style

Helga's brow game has always been on point, but even she knows the pressure of conforming to society's beauty standards. So, next time you look in the mirror, channel this style icon.

1. Embrace your unibrow.
2. Stop caring what school bullies think.
3. Spam your social media pages with some self-confident selfies.

#BrowsOnFleek #MyStyleMyRules #Flawless

Keep it on the DL

You're crazier than Chocolate Boy on a juice cleanse if you think no one knows about your not-so-secret crush. Let's face it, everyone except clueless football heads can totally tell what's up.

EXHIBIT A: The involuntary noises you make every time they're around you.
EXHIBIT B: The heart-shaped locket you recite poetry to on a near-hourly basis.

#SorryNotSorry #Obvious #IShipIt

"He doesn't get it! He doesn't know my secret! . . . He still can't even tell that I adore him. Oh, my football-headed love god!"

Helga Pataki: "Helga on the Couch," Season 4, Episode 16 (December 1999)

Arnold: "Cover me, Gerald!"
Gerald: "I'm watching your backside, Romeo."

Arnold Shortman and Gerald Johanssen: "Arnold's Valentine," Season 1, Episode 20
(February 1997)

Rely on your wingman

So you want to impress that cutie at the party, but you're feeling anxious? Let your wingman get you hyped and boost your confidence by talking you up in front of the object of your affections. You'll soon be ready to fly solo.

weird thumbshake

#HeyBuddy   #Bromance   #BFFs

Getting a date

First impressions are key, so you need
to make your crush see the real you.
(Let's face it, the social-media-friendly you
isn't fooling anyone with your workout selfies
and salad pics.) And if your date turns out to
be un-bae-lievably judgmental because they
"don't date short people" or whatever,
call them out on their attitude.

#TrueToYourself #DatingIsHard

"I promise you I'm a nice guy and I really think I could show you a good time, maybe a few laughs. So what do you say, huh?"

Ernie Potts: "Ernie in Love," Season 5, Episode 7 (April 2000)

"I think you're . . . okay. I mean, you're an okay guy and I just think you're okay."

Helga Pataki: "Monkey Business," Season 2, Episode 5 (October 1997)

Play hard to get

It's basic schoolyard logic: play hard to get and make bae want you—NOT the other way around. The last thing you want is your crush seeing red flags and ghosting you. FYI, mistaking a minor allergic reaction for a deadly disease and using it as an excuse to declare your love = too extra.

#Chillax #TreatThemMean #SoExtraItHurts

Making the first move

Spoiler: People tend not to like
being forced into a kiss.

Make sure you and your S.O. are in the same
headspace before sharing spit by straight-up
asking bae if they want to lock lips with you.

#NeverBeenKissed   #Desperate   #CanYouNot

"Give daddy some sugar!"

Thaddeus "Curly" Gammelthorpe: "Deconstructing Arnold," Season 4, Episode 9
(September 1999)

"Okay, so he doesn't *like me* like me. But he does like me, and that means I'm halfway there."

Helga Pataki: "Helga's Masquerade," Season 5, Episode 2 (March 2000)

Accept their feelings

As much as it hurts, your crush may not feel the same way about you. You can either remain a borderline stalker in your quest for love, or you can move on. Getting over someone is tough, but you can do it—and without needing to resort to any elaborate schemes. Looking at you, Helga . . . .

#GetOverIt   #EverHopeful   #OnToTheNext

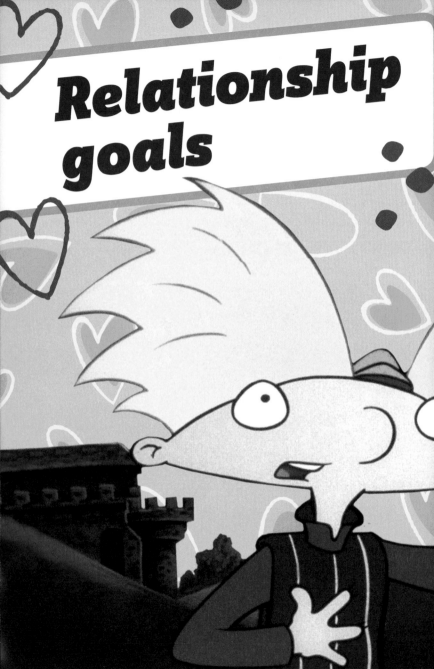

Relationship goals

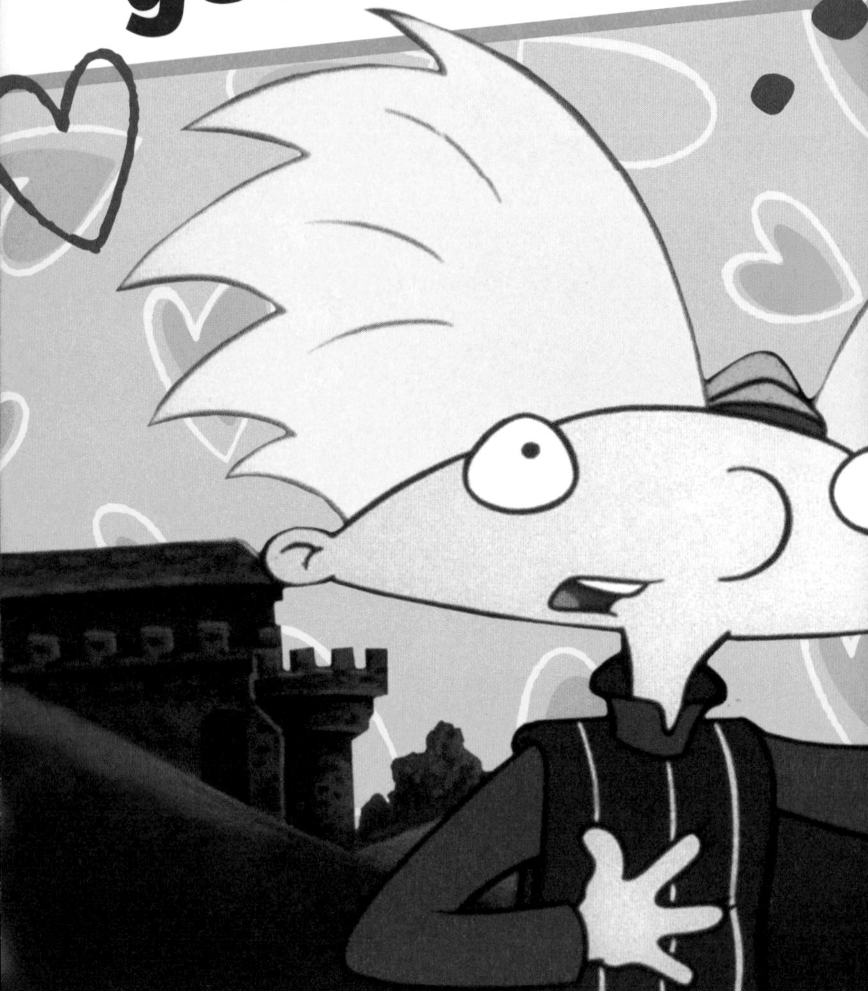

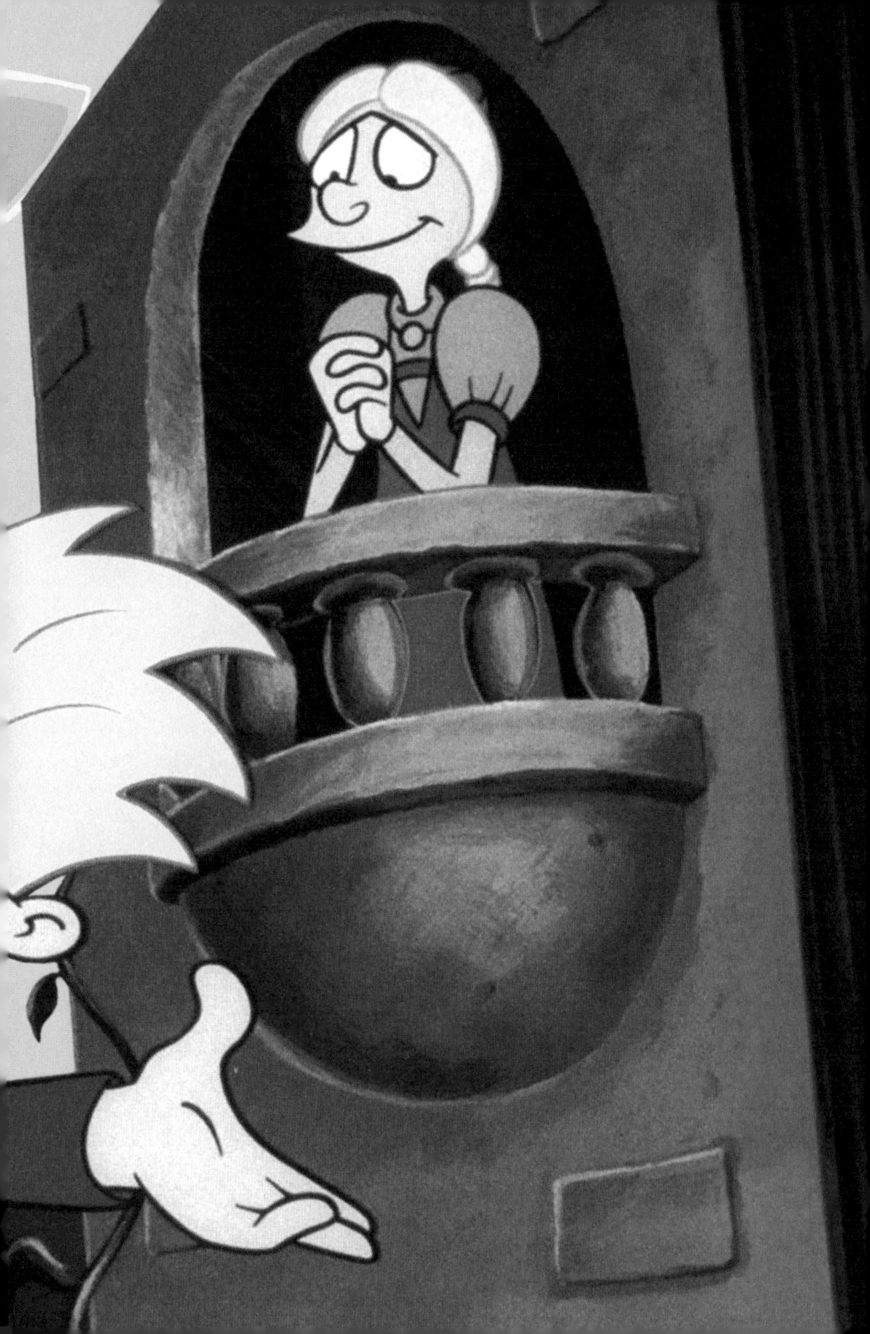

Love at first sight

We're not saying the hottie you just met and now insist you're head-over-heels in love with is DEFINITELY a con artist. What we're saying is it'd be good to get to know them before you start thinking about major life changes.

Pro tip: Make sure they're not already married.

#TrustNoOne #Facts #BoyBye

Helga: "So how long have you two known each other?"
Olga: "Three weeks and two days."

Helga and Olga Pataki: "Olga Gets Engaged," Season 3, Episode 5 (September 1998)

"I think we should spend as much time together as possible, don't you?"

Lila Sawyer: "Arnold and Lila," Season 3, Episode 13 (November 1998)

Define the relationship

So you've been getting to know someone super low-key, but now you want to step it up a level. Be confident like sixth-grader Lila, sit your S.O. down, and tell them what you want out of this relationship. You'll soon figure out if they like you or if they *like you* like you.

#KnowYourWorth #LikeLike #DTR

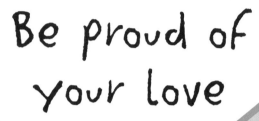

Be proud of your love

If someone's dissing your boo or your relationship, don't go crying to your mommy. Snap as many selfies as you want, post as many kiss pics as you please, and make date night as sickeningly sweet as cotton candy. Haters gonna hate.

#TotesAdorbs #KissPic #JustJealous

"Why do I care what you think?
The only thing that matters is what I think.
And what I think is I like Patty!"

Harold Berman: "Hey Harold!" Season 3, Episode 11 (October 1998)

Oskar: "Suzie, make me a sandwich!"
Suzie: "In a minute Oskar, I'm ironing your pants."

Oskar and Suzie Kokoshka: "Baby Oskar," Season 4, Episode 11 (October 1999)

Share the load

Relationships are a two-way street, meaning you can't let your love work 24/7 while you lounge around the apartment and expect to be treated like royalty. Putting bae's needs in second place to your own is not "pretty good," regardless of what Oskar might say.

#MarriedLife   #Equality   #MakeAnEffort

Be loyal to your love

Hooking up with someone who's already in a relationship may seem like a good idea at the time, but it'll end with one or both of you getting hurt. Do be like Arnold and stand your ground. Don't be like Lulu and poach your bae's family members.

#NoSecrets   #StayClassy   #StandByYourMan

Lulu: "I'm certain that I'm trying to kiss you."
Arnold: "Kiss me?! But you're Arnie's girlfriend! And we're nine!"

Arnold Shortman and Lulu: "Arnold Visits Arnie," Season 5, Episode 12 (January 2001)

"I want to grow up having a fabulous life, traveling around the world with him! Coffee in Paris, roses, sailboats, the whole nine yards."

Helga Pataki: "Helga on the Couch," Season 4, Episode 16 (December 1999)

Dream big

Good things come to those who wait, but GREAT things come to those who go and get them. Be vocal in your desires or expectations for your relationship. And if it isn't working out? Never settle for less than you deserve. Tighten that hairbow, smooth that dress, and keep moving forward.

#ExpressYourself   #LifeGoals   #ThisGirlCan

In the doghouse

Love isn't all sunshine and rainbows and free treats from the Jolly Olly Ice Cream truck. You're going to hit snags in any relationship, and that's okay. You need to communicate your feelings, but also listen when your partner drops some hard truths.

#RoughPatch   #DontBeSelfish   #UseYourWords

"But Suzie, where am I going to sleep?"

Oskar Kokoshka: "Arnold as Cupid," Season 1, Episode 12 (November 1996)

Bob: "Get married in a year, if you still want to . . . ."
Miriam: "You won't want to."

Miriam and Robert "Big Bob" Pataki: "Olga Gets Engaged," Season 3, Episode 5 (September 1998)

Make the magic last

Anyone who tells you marriage is easy is wackier than one of Grandpa Phil's war stories. Making a relationship last past the honeymoon stage is tough and requires your full devotion. Turn off your work email, give meal-prepping a rest, and ask your S.O. about their day for a change.

#TheStruggleIsReal   #MarriageMaterial

Couple goals

Getting into crazy shenanigans with your pookie sounds way more fun than holding a grudge because they left the cap off the toothpaste. To make a relationship last, you have to accept people for who they are, even if that includes them occasionally cosplaying as a cat.

#OldMarriedCouple   #Pookie   #2gether4eva

"You might get stuck with this girl for a long time, so you better try and make peace."

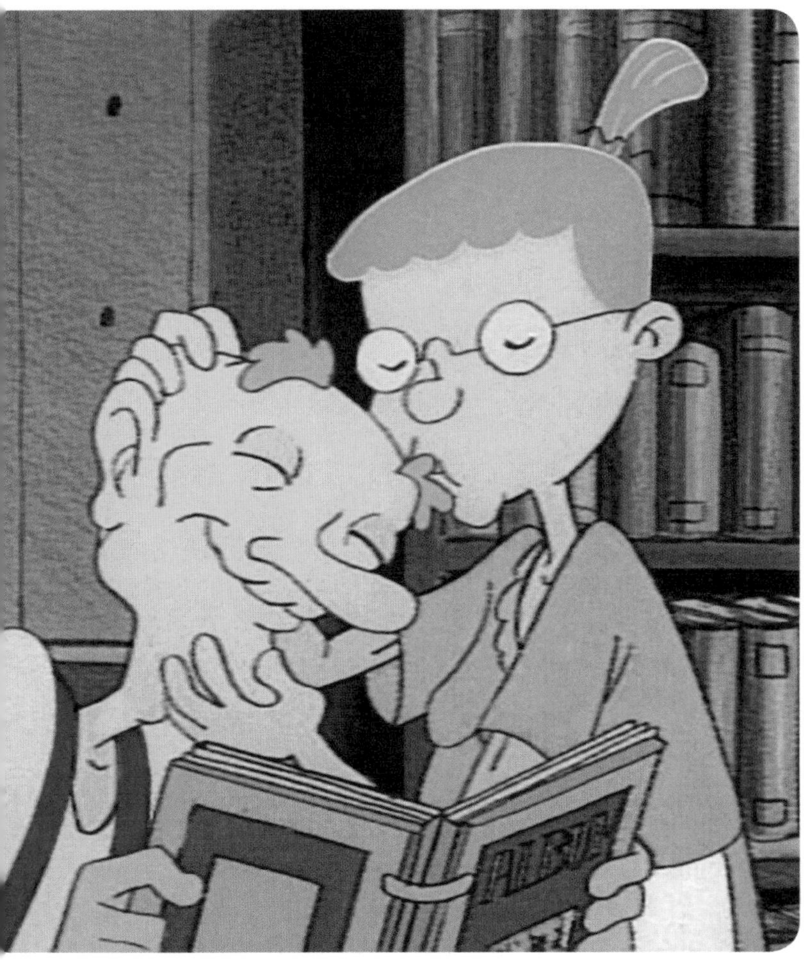

Grandpa Phil: "Girl Trouble," Season 3, Episode 19 (January 1999)

Love is tough

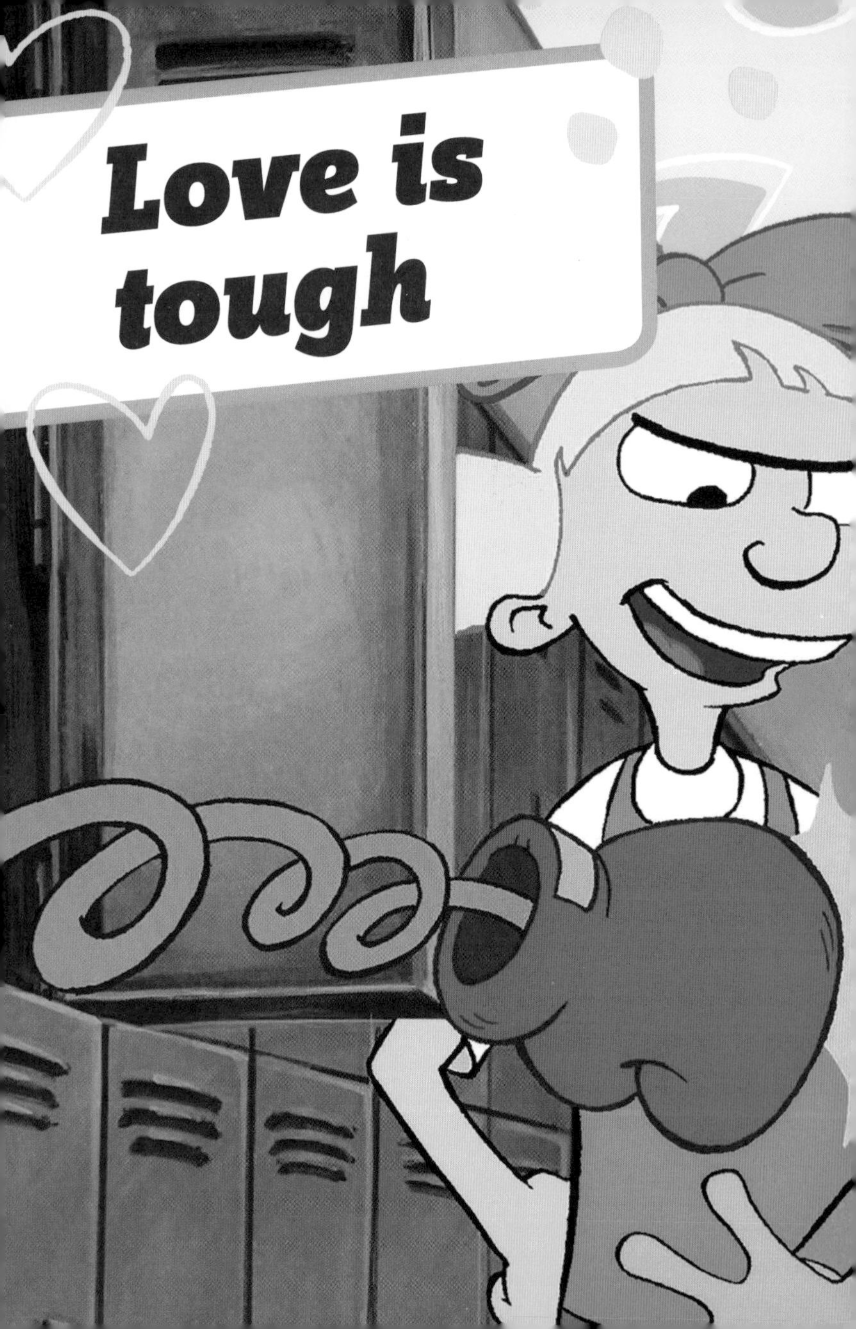

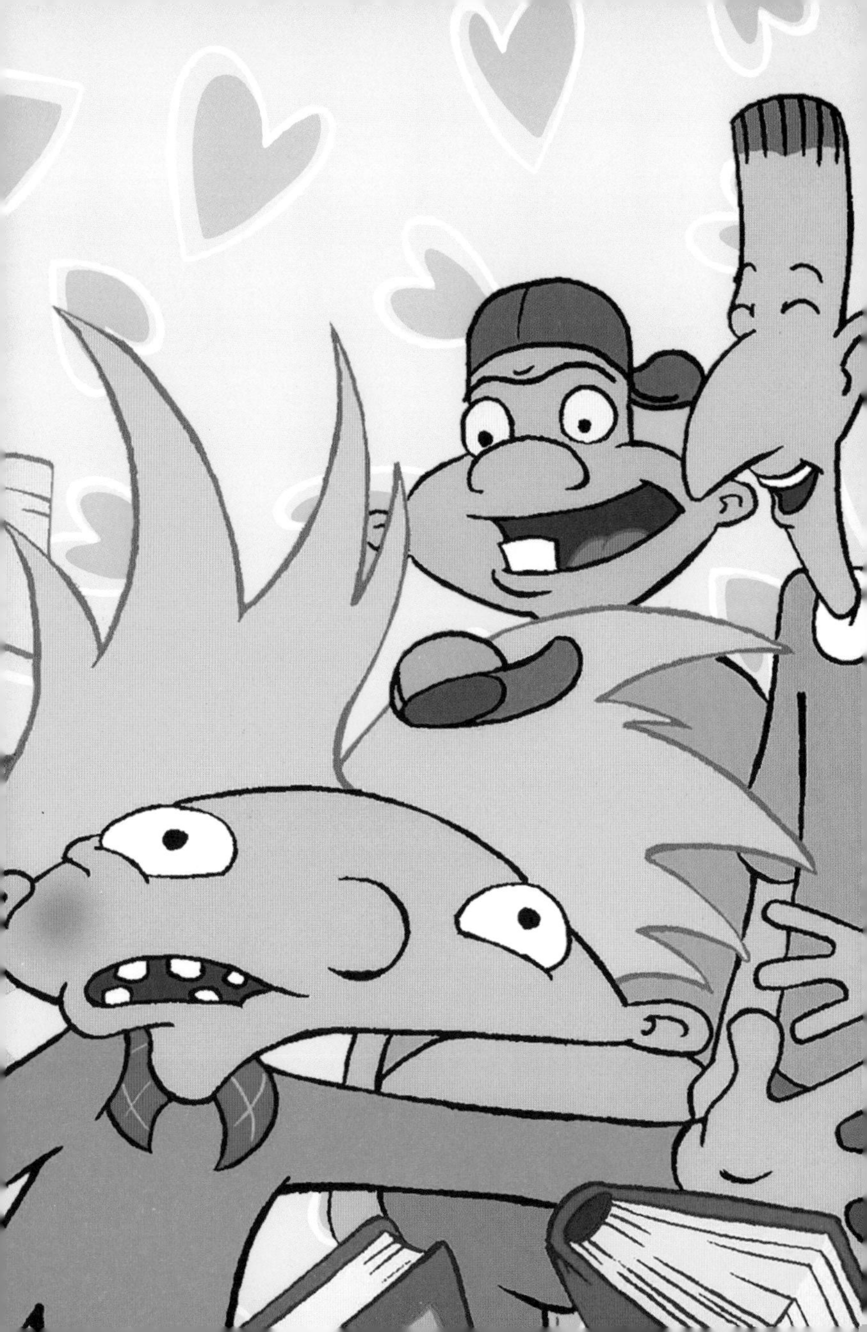

“I don’t want to go into the Tunnel of Love with you, Rhonda!”

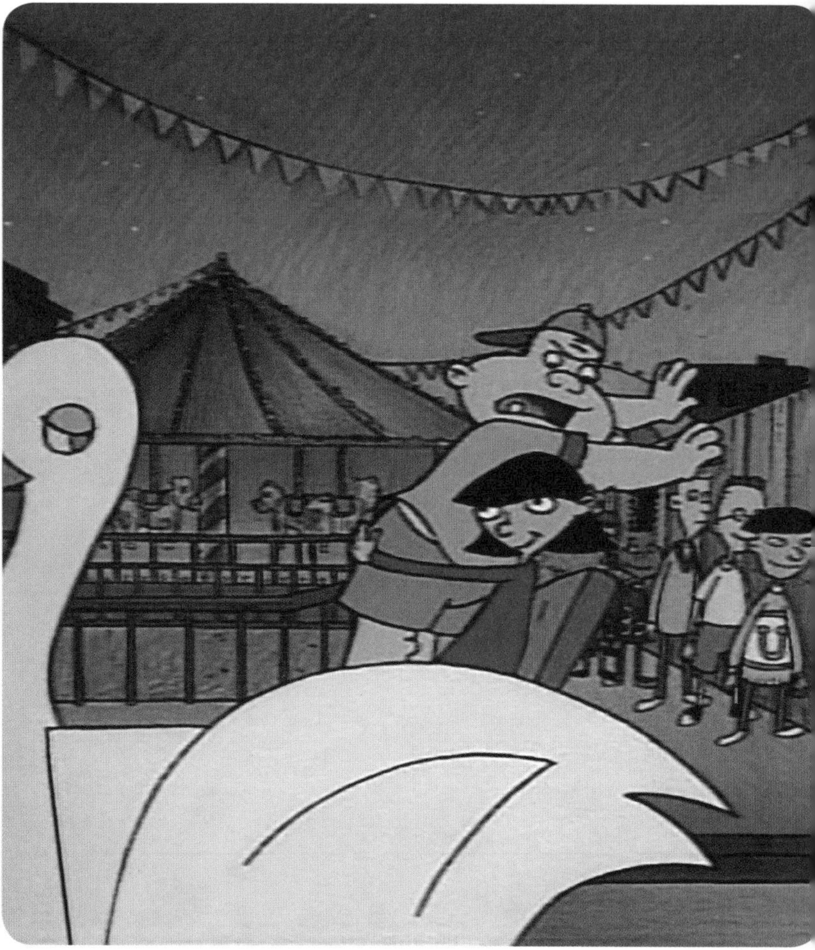

Harold Berman: “Operation Ruthless,” Season 1, Episode 7 (November 1996)

Take no for an answer

Even if all you can think about is riding through the Tunnel of Love with your crush, don't force the issue. Manhandling bae onto a swanboat like Rhonda isn't the answer. You might find there are people already lining up to take their place . . . .

#BeCool #KeepYourOptionsOpen

Difficult conversations

Sometimes, you have to be blunt to get rid of unwanted attention from someone with a crush. You can take the Helga approach and smack that mouth breather between the eyes (not recommended), or you can go the Lila route and be polite but firm.

#SpeakYourMind #ShutDown #SorryNotSorry

"You and I are really good friends and all but, as I've told you oh so many times, I just don't *like you* like you."

Lila Sawyer: "Weird Cousin," Season 4, Episode 11 (October 1999)

"He's pathetic. He's in love with me. I could probably get him to build me five sandcastles."

Summer: "Summer Love (a.k.a. Beach Story)," Season 5, Episode 9 (June 2000)

Drop the players

Know your self-worth and don't let anyone use your sparkle for their own winning-a-sandcastle-competition agenda. Stand up for yourself and let the person know you're not a doormat. Who cares if they're a hot, older wannabe-actress you met at the beach? You have standards.

#Respect   #SpringBreak   #KnowYourWorth

Don't get obsessed

Thanks to modern technology, it's easier than ever to vet your potential dates online. But when you start building a life-size model of them out of used gum, it may be time to dial it back and chill out. Find a happy medium for your adoration—journaling, maybe?

#ILYSM   #NoChill   #RelationshipGoals

"Why must I hold you only whilst I dream?
Will I forever be enslaved by your spell?"

Helga Pataki: "Helga's Parrot," Season 4, Episode 6 (April 1999)

"He's so right. It would have been unfair for me to expect to keep him to myself."

Olga Pataki: "Olga Gets Engaged," Season 3, Episode 5 (September 1998)

Dealing with a broken heart

While breakups are the worst, they can help you realize the kind of person you truly want to be with (and can also weed out liars and cheaters). Whether you've been ghosted by an online date or jilted at the altar, it'll take some time to process your emotions, but remember everything happens for a reason.

#Heartbreaker   #RightInTheFeels   #BetterAlone

Learning to trust again

When you take a chance on someone, sometimes you get hurt. That's okay. What's not okay is letting rejection overwhelm you until you shut out everything but pigeons using you for free food. Wallow away, but you have to try and deal with those feels without totally turning your back on humanity.

#TrustIssues #Mood #ForeverAlone

"Some people are meant to be with people. And others like me are just different."

Pigeon Man: "Pigeon Man," Season 1, Episode 14 (November 1996)

"Boyfriend? I will never, ever have anything to do with you, Curly, ever!"

Rhonda Wellington Lloyd: "Curly's Girl," Season 5, Episode 18 (October 2002)

Never say never

Just because you don't see someone being what Current You needs right now doesn't mean Future You won't think differently. One day that pesky bro is spamming you with annoying dog filter selfies you ignore, the next you're doing the tango at the club. Life's wild sometimes.

#TheOne #MrRightNow #TakesTwoToTango

Find some closure

After a friend's breakup: You can move on—you're a strong, independent person. After your own breakup: Life is terrible. I should take an anti-love potion so I never feel again.

There's not a detox tea in the world that can heal a broken heart. Try self-care, dates with your squad, and some time out of the game.

#TreatYoSelf   #MySquad   #TableForOnePlease

"I want to be out of love. Is that possible?"

Helga Pataki: "Helga's Love Potion," Season 2, Episode 2 (September 1997)

Senior Editor Tori Kosara
Editor Beth Davies
US Editor Kayla Dugger
Designers Sam Bartlett and Rhys Thomas
Design Assistant James McKeag
Pre-Production Producer Marc Staples
Producer Lloyd Robertson
Managing Editor Paula Regan
Managing Art Editor Jo Connor
Art Director Lisa Lanzarini
Publisher Julie Ferris
Publishing Director Simon Beecroft

Dorling Kindersley would also like to thank Alexandra Maurer, James Salerno, and the wonderful team at Nickelodeon; Steve Crozier, Chris Gould, and Anna Pond for design assistance, and Allison Singer for editorial help.

First American Edition, 2018
Published in the United States by DK Publishing
345 Hudson Street, New York, New York 10014

Page design copyright © 2018 Dorling Kindersley Limited
DK, a Division of Penguin Random House LLC

18 19 20 21 22 10 9 8 7 6 5 4 3 2 1

001–313290–Oct/2018

nickelodeon™

Published in Great Britain by Dorling Kindersley Limited.

A catalog record for this book is available from the Library of Congress.

ISBN 978-1-4654-7551-0

DK books are available at special discounts when purchased in bulk for sales promotions, premiums, fund-raising, or educational use. For details, contact:
DK Publishing Special Markets, 345 Hudson Street, New York, New York 10014
SpecialSales@dk.com

Printed and bound in China

A WORLD OF IDEAS:
SEE ALL THERE IS TO KNOW

www.dk.com
www.nick.com